fast fun & easy®
BOOK COVER ART

Add a Quilted Fabric Touch to Binders,
Scrapbooks, Journals & More

Jake Finch

Wedding Keepsake Album by Becky Berg

C&T PUBLISHING

Text © 2007 Jacqueline Lee Finch

Artwork © 2007 C&T Publishing, Inc.

Publisher: Amy Marson

Editorial Director: Gailen Runge

Acquisitions Editor: Jan Grigsby

Editor: Stacy Chamness

Technical Editors: Gayl Gallagher, Georgie Gerl

Copyeditor/Proofreader: Wordfirm Inc.

Cover Designer: Kristy K. Zacharias

Design Director/Book Designer: Kristy K. Zacharias

Illustrator: Tim Manibusan

Production Assistant: Kiera Lofgreen

Photography: C&T Publishing, Inc., unless otherwise noted

Published by C&T Publishing, Inc., P.O. Box 1456, Lafayette, CA 94549

Finch, Jake.

Fast, fun & easy book cover art : add a quilted fabric touch to binders, scrapbooks, journals & more / Jake Finch.

 p. cm.

 ISBN-13: 978-1-57120-393-9 (paper trade : alk. paper)

 ISBN-10: 1-57120-393-1 (paper trade : alk. paper)

 1. Quilting. 2. Miniature quilts. 3. Book covers. I. Title. II. Title: Fast, fun, and easy book cover art.

 TT835.F542 2007

 746.46—dc22

                                        2006012913

Printed in China

10 9 8 7 6 5 4 3 2 1

dedication

This book—my first—is for Stephen, who told me so.

acknowledgments

None of us lives in a sealed environment, separated from the influence of other people. I know this and I pray that I don't miss anyone here. I'd like to thank:

The staff at C&T who turned a vision into a beautiful book, especially Stacy Chamness, Gayl Gallagher, Jan Grigsby, Kiera Lofgreen, Amy Marson, Luke Mulks, Gailen Runge, and Kristy Zacharias

My oldest friends, Sarah DiFrenna, who showed me life could be normal, and Kathy Ruppert, who gives me loyalty and laughter

Our wonderful friends who inspire, encourage, and take care of me and my family: The Akers, Bentleys, Blasers, Boes, Dawsons, Carters, Conns, Hoffmans, Flitsches, Keenes, Meyers, Nicholases, Romanellis, Slivas, Waldrons, Julia Hook, Nicole Land, and Carol Wilkinson: Thank you for your love and support

My quilting buds: Becky Berg, Peggy Eichhorn, Sandy Harper, Kim Heier, Mary Hill, Sam Hunter, Marie Jenkins, Phyllis Jones, Laurie Maas, Kerin Martin, Chris McDonald, Beth Perry, Dorothy Ryburn, Lynn Shortt, Annie Toth, Vicki Tymczyszyn, and Barbara Witman— thank you for your endless help and creative endeavors

Linda Johansen for creating such wonderful bowls and boxes that in turn inspired my own Cover Art creations

My sisters, brothers, nieces, nephews, aunts, uncles, and my many zany, wonderful cousins who make life interesting and fun

My grandmothers who taught me to never have idle hands or heart—I miss you terribly

My great aunt Edith, for your wisdom, comfort, and absolutely unconditional love

My dads, who gave me the precious gift of words, one through writing, the other through reading

My mom, who always believes and takes great joy in who I am, gives me boundless love, and sees only the best in me

My husband and daughter: Stephen, you are my other half. Samantha, you are our result, what we take for ourselves and what we leave for the world, thank you for sharing your wife and mommy

And the Lord, through whom all is possible

contents

Imagine

in the beginning

Cover Art book covers were born from an obsession of mine—personal organizer books. A fan of Franklin-Covey, I had a planner that used an insert binder in a leather cover. I wanted to make my binder a new home. How could I use my quilting skills, without settling for the flimsy nature of a typical quilted cover or the bulk of inside seams? Heavyweight interfacing was the answer. It provides a stable edge that, when stitched properly, holds together the several layers of fabric and batting needed to make the cover without requiring the piece to then be turned right side out.

The basic techniques are simple and can be adapted to any type of cover project. Once the techniques are mastered, the variations on the beginning form are endless. Cover Art book covers can become your own practical works of quilt art. They are fun experiments with fabric and doodads. They also make great gifts that can be easily customized to the tastes and interests of the recipient.

My goal is to offer you the direction needed to learn the Cover Art techniques and then to have you launch into your own creative universe. Make yours better than mine. I know you can. Then spread your Cover Art around to others!

I hesitate to share the size of my quilt, scrap, paper art, and craft library with you for fear of spousal retri-

bution. But I will say that whenever I feel stalled, there are enough visual examples of other people's work to stimulate my own flow back to success. I can't count the number of magazines that cater to the crafting audience, and each one can be tapped for ideas. I use the layout sections of scrapbook magazines, blocks from quilt magazines, card-making magazines that show how to make a big impact with a small package, and photography publications that offer studies in color and composition as well as springboards for photo transfer opportunities.

Another wonderful source of creativity can be found in museums. Art museums, natural history museums, even auto museums all provide examples of design and composition. Find what you like, what catches your eye, or what makes you think, and translate it into fabric and fiber.

The best way to capture your inspiration is to always keep a sketchpad with you. Even a tiny notebook will prove handy as ideas pop into your mind at the least appropriate moments. It will take only a couple of words or lines scribbled onto your pad to serve as a reminder of what held your imagination when you look at it later.

And, finally, be sure to honor copyright laws. Generally, if something was designed, photographed, or written by someone else, that person probably holds the copyright. You need written permission from the creator before using his or her materials in a project that might provide you with financial gain, or you may violate that individual's copyright. Be careful and be respectful of other people's creations. There are plenty of public-domain, copyright-free quotes, photographs, and quilt patterns that you can use.

materials, tools & techniques

Cover Art covers were born from my obsession with quilting.

Basic Materials

things to cover

When just starting out with your covers, stick to books and binders with covers that are firm but not too thick. For instance, a journal with a thickly padded cover will become too bulky when covered with more layers of fabric and batting. Feel free to experiment. Find a need and fill it. How can you go wrong with such small commitments of fabric, money, and time?

There are so many things out there that you can cover with art!

One note about how the project instructions were written: due to the unknown dimensions of what you choose to cover, all yardages are estimated with the expectation of leftovers. Unless you begin with the exact same binder or book to cover, your finished project will not be just like mine.

fabric

To me, each cover is a miniature work of quilt art. Because of this, I have mostly stuck with good-quality 100% cotton quilt fabrics, with some fancies such as velvet and silk thrown in, to make the covers. Don't discount decorator prints or designer woolens, but when using them, always account for the fabric's weight, what needle you will use, whether any stabilizer will be needed for more delicate fabrics, and what the final thickness of your cover will be.

Fabrics—the hard part is choosing.

interfacing

My favorite option is fast2fuse double-sided interfacing, made by C&T Publishing (see Sources, page 48). This product comes in two different weights and has the added bonus of being a double-sided fusible. The instructions in *Fast, Fun & Easy Book Cover Art* are all written using fast2fuse, but if you need to substitute a nonfusible interfacing, make sure to have an equal amount of fusible web on hand to bond the lining fabric to your inside cover.

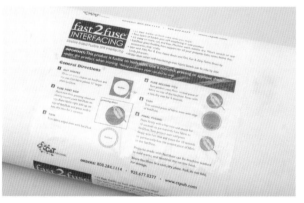

fast2fuse—a wonderful option for your covers' interfacing

easy!

To avoid creases, buy interfacing from the bolt when possible.

basting spray

I swear by 505 Spray and Fix (see Sources, page 48). This temporary spray adhesive is used for basting quilts or holding appliqué pieces in place. It leaves almost no gummy residue on needles. It is stainless, odorless, and acid free—a mandatory requirement for products used in scrapbooking. Follow the manufacturer's instructions. Use it in a well-ventilated area and don't ever confuse it with spray starch, as I once did while ironing my favorite denim shirt.

fusible web

What you want to remember when choosing a fusible web is to find a lightweight, permanent product. With all the other layers involved in making your cover, you want the least amount of added bulk possible for smooth sewing. I use Steam-a-Seam 2 (see Sources, page 48). It comes in large rolls and allows for repositioning of the fabric before you permanently bond it with an iron.

thread

I love the effect thread can add to an otherwise simple piece of fabric or quilt block. The trick with using any thread beyond your standard cotton is to know what needle it works best with. Ask your quilt shop owner, look it up in one of the many books on machine quilting and thread use on the market, or refer to the thread manufacturer's website. The joy of Cover Art is that your imagination is let loose on a relatively small piece of canvas. So experiment with those beautiful, shiny threads calling to you.

Play with the many glorious types of decorative threads on the market.

I enjoy using Robison-Anton's rayon thread for my edge stitching (see Sources, page 48). The thread works well in my machine, offers an elegant finish, and is sturdier than other types of rayon thread. Like the binding on a finished quilt, your edge stitching should not be the dominant visual effect of your finished cover. I save variegated threads for topstitching and quilting, and use a complementary solid for both top and bobbin threads.

When embellishing your covers with things that will be sewn on, use a good-quality invisible thread. I use YLI Wonder Invisible Thread (see Sources, page 48). I've found that this brand tangles the least and moves smoothly through my needle. I've recently discovered Libby Lehman's Bottom Line thread, made by Superior Threads (see Sources, page 48). This ultra-fine, ultra-strong polyester thread can be used on your bobbin for quilting and satin stitching, but not for edge stitching.

batting

Because you will be quilting through a two-layer sandwich, your batting choice is very important to your machine's well-being. Choose a batting that is needle-punched and thin. My choice is The Warm Company's Warm & Natural or Warm & White (see Sources, page 48). When using it, make sure the needle-punched side is facing the feed dogs. It will shed the least and therefore lint up your machine less. Clean your machine after quilting your batting-and-fabric sandwich.

anti-fray liquids

Loose threads can be easily tamed with a dot of some kind of anti-fray liquid. Those products made for fabrics—Fray Check or FrayBlock, for instance (see Sources, page 48)—dry clear, are acid free, and are washable.

photo transfer papers & fabrics

Many types of photo transfer products are available to personalize your projects.

Incorporating photos into your covers is a wonderful way to personalize your efforts. Special papers can be run through your computer's ink-jet printer to put photographs onto iron-transfer paper. There are also fabrics specially treated and sized to run through your printer so that you can print a photo directly onto the fabric. There are even chemicals available, such as Bubble Jet Set 2000 (see Sources, page 48), that enable you to make your own photo fabric sheets.

As with interfacings, it is essential that you follow the manufacturer's instructions completely when using transfer media, whether paper or fabric.

Tools

rotary cutters, mats & rulers

You'll need a medium-sized rotary cutter with extra blades for the projects.

Rotary cutter mats are self-healing, are printed with a 1″ grid, and have marks at ⅛″ intervals. A mat that's at least 18″ × 24″ should take you through almost any size cover.

Quilter's rulers come in a huge assortment of sizes and colors. In general they are made from clear Lucite and are marked with grid lines spaced at least ¼″ apart. You will need at least two to comfortably make most Cover Art projects. Use a 6″ × 24″ or 8″ × 24″ as your main ruler and a 12″ or 12½″ square as a backup ruler.

Another very useful ruler that I use is a 12″ T-square. There's nothing fancy about this ruler except that it has a lip that can run along the clean edge of your cover, providing a stable edge from which to measure. You can live without it, but life is so much easier with it.

If you are approaching Cover Art from a scrapbooker's perspective, you will soon be converted to these quilter's tools because of the ease with which they accomplish the job of cutting accurately and quickly. The initial investment may seem a little steep if you don't already have these tools on hand, but they will pay for themselves many times over.

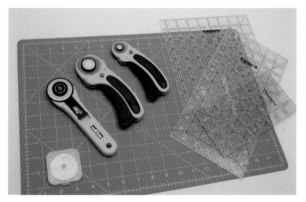

Rotary tools work well for all types of crafts.

glue gun

I've had great success using a standard glue gun and glue sticks to bond metal doodads and other things to my Cover Art. You don't need a fancy glue gun—a small one will work perfectly. Just be careful not to leave strings of glue on your covers.

iron & accessories

Any type of steam iron will work, just make sure when you're ironing your fusible products that you have read the manufacturer's instructions thoroughly, as some products require steam and others don't.

You will also need a nonstick ironing surface when working with fusibles to protect your ironing board cover.

pens

You will need only two permanent fine-line markers, one in red and one in black, for all the projects.

sewing machine & accessories

Sewing machines can be as unique as the people who operate them. In my classes I've seen an enormous range of machines, and so far I've never lost a Cover Art project due to a machine.

That said, what your machine really needs to be able to do is to create a tight satin stitch and to sew through bulky, heavyweight fabrics. Most modern machines will perform these tasks with the proper needles and thread.

One accessory that might help greatly is an overcast foot. This foot takes a zigzag foot a step further by giving your thread a support to rest on as you're zigzagging along an edge. Some manufacturers call this foot an *edger*.

One type of overcast foot used for edge stitching

Another machine accessory you'll rely on for certain tasks is the zipper foot. It allows the needle to run alongside an object (such as the sketch pencils in the sketchbook project).

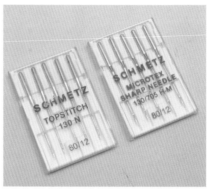

Don't hesitate to change a needle. The newer the needle, the better the stitching.

quilter's gloves

Any type of machine quilting is helped along immensely when you wear quilter's gloves. The gripper dots on these gloves provide traction against the fabric and are almost mandatory when aiming for frustrationless free-motion quilting.

needles

Sewing machine needles are probably your most important tool in making Cover Art. Because your machine is going to be working very hard punching through different layers and weights of materials, your needles will either enable or inhibit you from the start. I have had the best and most consistent luck with Schmetz brand topstitch needles (see Sources, page 48). All piecing and edge finishing on my Cover Art projects is done with either an 80/12 topstitch or 90/14 topstitch needle. For piecing the outside covers, I use Schmetz sharps, usually 80/12. I use one needle for each project and quickly change to a new needle at the first sign of trouble. If your thread starts breaking or your stitching seems sluggish, change your needle.

Practice on a sample before trying the finishing techniques on your covers. That way you can experiment until you get the right combination of needle and tension before even touching your final project.

decorating & embellishing

- ☐ Buttons
- ☐ Ribbons
- ☐ Decorative brads
- ☐ Metal stick-on scrapbook embellishments

- ☐ Yarn
- ☐ Charms
- ☐ Beads
- ☐ Rhinestones
- ☐ Stick-on cloth labels

- ☐ Polymer clay charms and buttons
- ☐ Shrink plastic charms and buttons
- ☐ Wire
- ☐ Costume jewelry

- ☐ Hat pins
- ☐ Stamps
- ☐ Stencils
- ☐ Fabric or acrylic paints
- ☐ Eyelets
- ☐ Grommets

covering
the basics

Regardless of how detailed your book cover ends up, each is made up of three main parts: the inside (called the main pattern piece), the sleeves, and the quilted outside. We'll take each part separately and then join them all together as our final step.

What You'll Need

- **Binder** For this first project, we'll cover a basic 3-ring binder that holds 8½″ × 11″ paper. Use a binder with a spine between 1″ and 3″ wide.

> Do not use a D-ring binder for this first project. Once you master the basics you'll be able to adapt the cover for the D-ring.

- **Fabric** 2 yards of something you love. If you want different fabrics for the three main parts, figure ½ yard for the quilted outside (show off a great fabric!), ½ yard for the inside lining (which will barely be seen), and 1 yard for the sleeves. These are generous estimates.

- **Regular or heavyweight fast2fuse interfacing** ½ yard. (If you're not using a fusible interfacing, you'll need the same amount of fusible web on hand to bond the interfacing to the fabric.)

- **Thread** About 500 yards of rayon thread for finishing edges. Can also be used for quilting the cover, or use other thread for that purpose.

- **Basic materials** See pages 6–10.

How-Tos

main pattern piece

1. Place the open loose-leaf binder on top of the unrolled fast2fuse. Do not bring the binder to the edges of the fast2fuse. Leaving at least 1″ of space around the binder, trace the outline of the cover onto the fast2fuse using a black marker.

Trace outline of binder onto interfacing.

easy!

> Save all fast2fuse scraps for small projects or for additions to your covers. Handles, tabs, bookmarks, and some dimensional projects are perfect uses.

2. Use a red marker and ruler to draw a ½″ seam allowance outside the bottom edge of the binder tracing. Be sure to make this first edge as straight as possible. It will be used to square off the other 3 edges. Cut along the red edge.

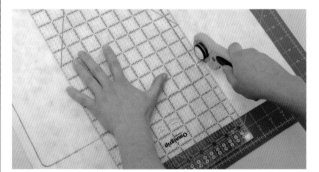

Make the first cut—be sure it's straight!

3. The bottom edge is now your guide for the top edge. Take the red marker and rotary ruler (you might need to use 2 rulers to square off the edge; see the photo below) and draw a ½″ seam allowance outside the top edge of the cover parallel to the lower edge already made.

Square off the second side using two rulers.

4. Cut along the red line with the rotary cutter.

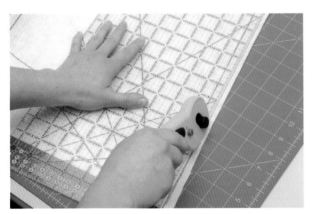

Cutting the second side

Don't mark the sides yet. We first need to allow for the cover's ease.

5. To finish the side edges, center the open 3-ring binder back on the main pattern piece, lining up the top and bottom edges on the black tracing. Slowly close the cover while carefully wrapping the main pattern piece around it.

Wrap the main fast2fuse piece around the binder, allowing for ease in the finished cover. Mark the side edges.

6. Use the red marker to make a small mark at each edge where the cover ends. You'll probably see that these marks will increase the width of the cover's edges. This extra space is called the *ease* and gives the cover enough room to move.

7. With the ruler, draw red edge lines where each small mark is, using the top and bottom edges to square off each side of the main pattern piece. Repeat for the opposite side.

Square off edges before trimming.

8. With the rotary cutter, cut ½″ away from the red edge line on each side.

This is your **main pattern piece** for the book cover. It will be used in the construction of the cover and also as a guide for the other parts of the cover.

easy!

If the corners of the cover are rounded, don't worry about squaring them off. We will address rounded corners soon (page 17).

fold lines & cover lining

1. Center the open binder on the main pattern piece. Make a small mark at the bottom of the binder where each side will bend.

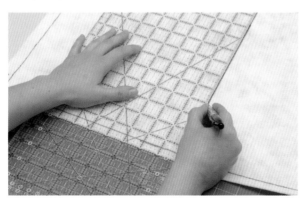

Mark the fold lines.

2. Take the ruler, square up the bottom edge, and draw 2 black marker lines, 1 along each fold line, from the bottom mark to the top edge of the cover. If you have one, this is where the T-square ruler is really helpful.

Draw fold lines from bottom to top.

3. Draw more black lines, about every ¼″, in the space between the 2 fold lines and 1 line ¼″ away from the outside of each fold line.

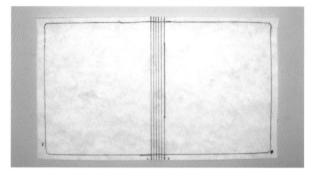

Draw additional fold lines.

4. Place the ironed lining fabric wrong side up on the table. Place the main pattern piece, marked side up, on the fabric along the selvage width.

5. With the markings facing up, roughly cut around the main pattern piece.

Roughly cut lining fabric around fast2fuse main pattern piece.

6. Bring both pieces together to the ironing board and fuse the lining fabric to the unmarked side of the main pattern piece. Place a nonstick pressing sheet under the marked side of the main pattern piece when pressing.

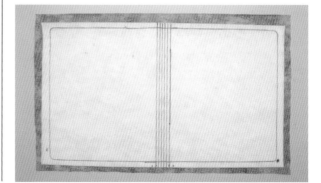

Fuse lining fabric to main pattern piece.

7. Trim the fabric to the edge of the main pattern piece.

8. Stitch along each marked fold line. Watch the stitch tension on the fabric side, adjusting as needed.

easy!

Don't skip the fold lines. Without them, the stiff interfacing will have a mind of its own. Add more if needed. They are hidden in the finished cover.

sleeves for the inside cover

1. Center the open binder on the unlined side of the main pattern piece. Make a small mark along the bottom edge where the cover sleeve needs to extend to. Remove the binder. Mark as close to the folds of the cover as possible without covering them.

Make small marks where the edge of the sleeve ends.

2. Cut a piece of sleeve fabric about twice the width of the closed binder and 2″ longer than the binder length. Fold the sleeve fabric in half, wrong sides together. Press the fold line straight and flat.

3. With the fold facing the inside of the cover, place the folded edge of the sleeve on top of the lined side of the main pattern piece. Use a ruler or T-square to square off the sleeve edge at the mark just made.

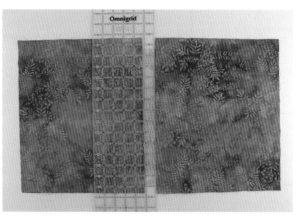

Line up sleeves using your rotary ruler and mat. A T-square also works well.

4. Carefully pin the sleeves in place at the corners, making sure the sleeves don't shift or pucker.

fast!

If the edge of the sleeve needs reinforcement for frequent removal of your book cover, fuse the inside fold line of the sleeve edge with a strip of Steam-a-Seam 2 or Stitch Witchery (see Sources, page 48) for added stability.

5. With the marked side facing up and being careful of the pins on the back, carefully baste stitch the sleeves to the main pattern piece, about ⅛″ from the edge, making sure the sleeves don't shift or pucker.

easy!

If the edges pucker during basting, iron the main pattern piece—sleeve side up—from the center outward.

Baste stitch ⅛″ around inside edge of cover to secure sleeves to lining.

6. Use your rotary cutter to carefully trim the sleeves to the edge of the main pattern piece. Be sure not to slice into the main pattern piece.

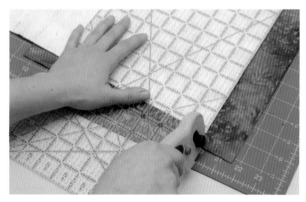

Trim sleeves to edges of main pattern.

making the quilted outside

1. Place the outside fabric, right side down, on the table. Place the batting on top of the fabric. Place the main pattern piece on the layered batting and fabric. Use your rotary ruler and cutter to cut the layered batting and fabric with a ½″ border around the main pattern piece.

Layer cover fabric, batting, and main pattern piece. Cut cover fabric and batting, leaving ½″ border around edges of main pattern piece.

easy!

If the batting you're using has a fluffy side and a smooth, needle-punched side, place the fluffy side down on the wrong side of your outside cover fabric to allow for easier quilting.

2. Separate the batting from the cover fabric and spray the wrong sides of each with spray baste. Layer the 2 spray-basted sides and smooth them together. If wrinkles appear on the fabric side, press it with an iron.

Spray baste cover fabric to batting, and quilt as desired.

3. Quilt as desired. When you're finished, iron the quilted piece.

fun!

You can outline stitch the motifs, or quilt an allover pattern. Even simple lines, especially using decorative threads, look great.

putting it all together

1. Spray baste the marked side of the main pattern piece and the batting side of the quilted outside.

Spray baste quilted cover and main pattern piece, lined side down.

2. Place the quilted outside, batting side up, on a firm surface. Carefully center the main pattern piece on top of the quilted outside, bonding the 2 spray-basted sides together. Smooth the joined pieces together firmly.

Firmly smooth the two sections together.

3. Use the stiff edge of the main pattern piece as a guide to carefully trim the quilted outside cover to the main pattern piece with a rotary cutter or scissors.

Trim quilted cover to edge of main pattern piece.

rounding the corner

While developing the Cover Art techniques, I found that rounded corners work best with satin stitching. Square corners require the stitching to stop and then start again, creating loose threads and easily frayed corners. If you choose to keep your corners square, use Fray Check to secure loose threads (see Sources, page 48).

1. Use the cap from the can of spray baste to trace the curve on the 4 corners of the cover using the black marker.

Caps make great circle templates!

2. With scissors, carefully cut through all the layers, following the traced curved line.

getting it together

You will be sewing around the edge of your cover at least twice with a tight satin stitch to permanently join all the pieces together. This technique is what makes working with fast2fuse so wonderful. For the best results, use the same thread for the top and bobbin threads. I've found that a solid rayon thread makes the cleanest choice.

fast!

Experiment beforehand on a practice piece of fast2fuse, batting, fabric, and the thread you will use on the cover to determine the best needle type and tension settings for your machine.

1. Start with a narrower satin stitch. On my machine, I set the stitch width to 5.0 and length to .30 for the first pass. If your machine isn't that exact, set the length at the *almost* shortest setting and width at the *almost* widest setting.

easy!

Start with a full bobbin. You should be able to finish one stitching pass with one full bobbin. Use a second full bobbin for your second pass.

2. Begin at a point on the back of the cover and with the inside cover facing up in the machine. Carefully stitch along the inside edge, taking care to round the corners accurately, binding the edges as you go. Finish back where you started and snip your threads.

Carefully satin stitch your edges. Two passes should do.

3. With a second full bobbin, readjust your stitch to the *shortest* length and *widest* width. On my machine I use a 7.0 width and a .20 length. Sew with the quilted outside facing up.

Your cover is now completed. With the front and back panels of the binder folded back, carefully slip the cover's sleeves over the 3-ring binder, and enjoy!

fun!

There are so many uses for a pretty covered binder! Household files, student notebooks, journals, magazine clipping holders, scrapbook covers, your kids' artwork files, project folders, business card holders . . . look for useful 3-ring inserts at your office supply store.

Variations

A. ***Stars & Stripes*** Vicki Tymczyszyn used leftover quilt blocks for her wedding album Cover Art. (She was married on the 4th of July!)

B. ***Windows*** Alice Moriya used a Cathedral Windows block adapted from Shelly Swanland's ***Cathedral Windows by Machine.***

C. ***All Cooped Up!*** Chicken-wire quilting keeps Barbara Greene Witman's chicken in check.

D. ***Photo Album for John (and Peep)*** Chris McDonald gets spooky with her Halloween-themed Cover Art.

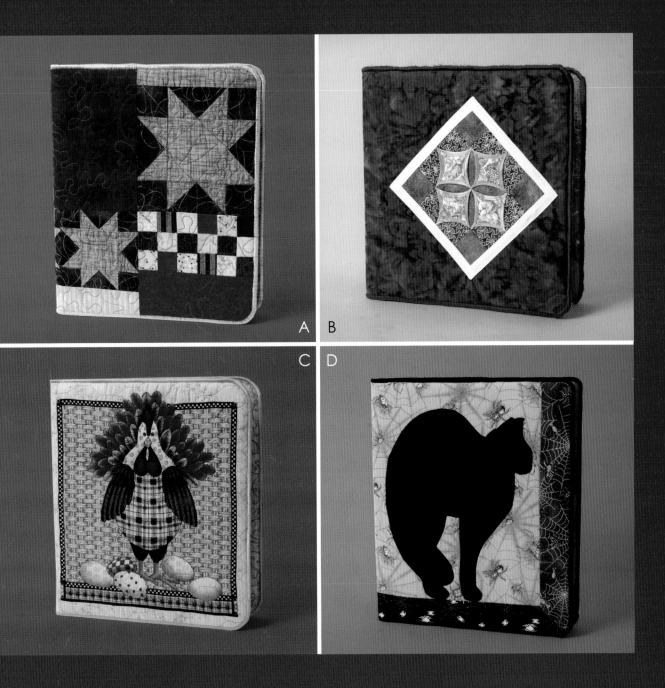

A B

C D

quick & easy
brag book

These little quilted jewels are perfect for gift giving. Shoot a roll of film of the kids and make several sets of copies to include in mini-scrapbooks—covered by you!—for gifts that family members will cherish.

What You'll Need

- [ ] 4″ × 6″ photo album—"brag book" style
- [ ] At least 3 different fat quarters or large fabric scraps
- [ ] ½ yard of lining and sleeve fabric
- [ ] ½ yard of regular fast2fuse (This will cover several brag books.)
- [ ] ½ yard of Steam-a-Seam 2 or other fusible bonding product
- [ ] Coordinating thread for edging
- [ ] Thread for piecing and quilting
- [ ] A great button for the closure
- [ ] A covered elastic ponytail holder
- [ ] Beads and buttons for embellishment
- [ ] Basic materials (See pages 6–10.)

The Fabric Formula for Brag Books

I have a down-and-dirty formula for making *Bragging Rights*. Mostly, I use three fabrics: a driving fabric, a calming fabric, and a diversion fabric. Their roles can change according to my mood and the final embellishments, but my motivation for choosing them remains.

Start with a really great fabric that tugs at your imagination, tickles your funny bone, or soothes your soul. This first fabric is your **driving fabric**, the one that drives you to your next fabric selection and on to one or two additional choices.

This pretty floral delighted me with its spunky use of red, so I picked it for my driving fabric.

One of your choices should be a **calming fabric**, one that can give your eye a rest and subtly highlight the personalities of the other fabrics. This could be a solid or near-solid fabric or a small, repetitive print without contrasting colors. It should not be a busy, color-filled print that will compete with your driving fabric.

The aqua and ivory polka dot works well because the dots are soft and blend in with the aqua.

My third choice is my **diversion fabric**. It's a fabric that can be an unexpected surprise that coordinates with the other two fabrics. The surprise could come from a color that is not likely to be immediately considered, a texture that wouldn't seem to readily blend with the others, or a print that speaks well for itself even though the viewer doesn't expect it to sing harmony with its partners as aptly as it does.

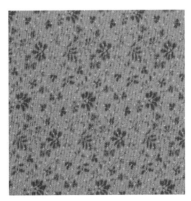

This sassy red-on-pink reproduction print makes me, and its partner fabrics, smile.

The same three fabrics used in different ways can completely change the look of your cover.

fast!

Brag books are readily available at craft stores and are generally very inexpensive. My favorite type is plastic with 24 pages bound in the center. I buy them by the dozens!

How-Tos

Because the technique for making the cover is the same as that for the basic book cover, I'll show variations on the cover design and the closures used for holding the book closed. These are simple ways to dress up your small cover quickly and effectively. Follow the instructions in Covering the Basics, Steps 1 through 8, on pages 12–13.

making the quilted outside

1. Choose a background fabric and follow the instructions for Making the Quilted Outside (page 16).

Quilting for these small covers should be subtle and easy.

easy!

Brag books require small amounts of fabric for their covers. So, less can be more. Choose simple quilting patterns such as loose squiggles, or straight or wavy lines. Thread also makes a big impact here, adding touches of shimmer or texture.

2. From the remaining 2 fabrics, pick a fabric to "shadow" the last fabric. This will be the fabric used the least. Cut a 3″ × 12″ strip of the shadow fabric and cover the back with fusible web. Then cut this piece into random squares and rectangles, each of a slightly different size. Set aside these pieces.

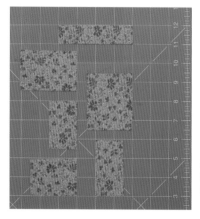

As a shadow fabric, the red will outline the last fabric.

3. From your last fabric cut a 4″ × 12″ strip and cover the back with fusible web. Then cut this piece into random squares and rectangles, again each of a slightly different size. Set aside these pieces.

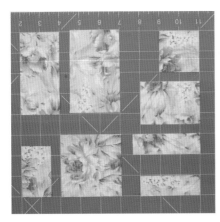

My driving fabric, the pretty floral, will stand out from the others in this arrangement.

4. Lay your quilted background down, right side up, and start placing the shadow cuts on top in whatever arrangement pleases you. Then add the other fabric cuts on top of the shadows. Move them around and experiment.

Play with your arrangements. The possibilities are endless!

5. When you've decided on the final pattern, carefully remove each piece, setting the pieces aside in a similar arrangement to what you've decided so you don't forget where to place them later.

6. Carefully peel the backing paper from each shadow piece, and press the pieces firmly to the quilted outside with your fingers.

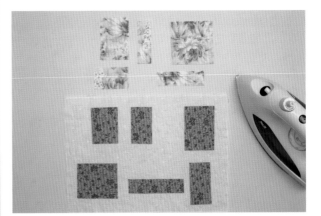

Lay out your pieces on the ironing board.

7. Fuse the shadow pieces to the quilted outside, following the manufacturer's instructions.

fast!

If you're using square and rectangular cuts that you want to make sure are lined up straight with the edges of the cover, use a rotary ruler or T-square ruler for accuracy.

8. Using any style stitch, stitch the inside edge of each piece for strength.

Stitching along the edge will help reinforce your fused pieces.

9. Repeat Steps 6 through 8 with the last fabric pieces, then embellish the cover as desired.

Try different decorative stitches for each set of cuts.

easy!

There is no way you'll use all your fused, cut pieces on one brag book, so save the unused ones in an envelope or other safe place. These are great for other projects.

button closure

Before joining the quilted outside to the main pattern piece, mark where the button will be sewn onto the outside of the quilted cover, with the top side up. Sew the button at this spot, using a scrap of interfacing on the backside for extra stability.

putting it all together

Follow the instructions in Putting It All Together on page 17, with one exception: after spray basting the quilted cover and lined main pattern piece, insert half of the ponytail holder between the quilted cover and the main pattern piece on the back of the cover where the holder will stretch over the button. The edge stitching will hold the ponytail holder in place.

rounding the corner

Follow the instructions on page 17.

Variations

A. **Small Photo Album** Chris McDonald harnessed solar power and used leaf sun prints.

B. **Deep Blue** The blue batik is the perfect "water" for these appliquéd fish.

A | B

checkbook cover
WITH BUTTON TIE & PENHOLDER

This is a quick and fun project, perfect for stocking stuffers or other small handmade gifts. This is a great project for using those fat quarters you're not sure what to do with. The penholder technique can be adapted to make pockets for your book covers—just enlarge the pocket to suit your needs!

What You'll Need

- ☐ A checkbook cover to use as a template (There is usually a plastic cover included in a box of checks.)
- ☐ A check register and a checkbook for marking the pattern
- ☐ ¼ yard of fast2fuse
- ☐ 3 fat quarters or ¼-yard cuts of coordinating fabrics for quilted cover, lining, and sleeves
- ☐ Coordinating thread for edging
- ☐ Thread for piecing and quilting
- ☐ A really cool 1″-wide button for the closure
- ☐ A covered elastic ponytail holder
- ☐ Basic materials (See pages 6–10.)

How-Tos

main pattern piece

Follow the instructions for the main pattern piece (on pages 12–13) through Step 6, with one exception: in Step 6, after you've marked the edges with the red pen and you're preparing to cut, add ½″ allowance to one short side and 1½″ to the other short side. (It doesn't matter which side you choose.) This will give you enough ease for the penholder.

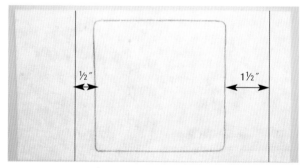

Mark 1½″ on one side to accommodate the penholder.

fold lines & cover lining

1. The fold line marks for the checkbook cover are placed in the center. Because you have allowed an extra inch in the center for the pen, fold the main pattern piece in half where the cover will fold when finished, and mark the exact center.

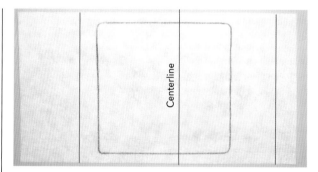

Mark your centerline.

2. Open and draw the centerline using your rotary ruler. Then draw lines from either side of the centerline, spaced about a ¼″ apart, for about ¾″ on each side.

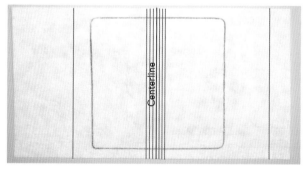

Mark your fold lines.

3. Continue following Fold Lines & Cover Lining, Steps 4 through 8, on pages 14–15.

sleeves for the inside cover

1. Because you're making a cover for 2 items—a checkbook and a check register—you'll need to mark the sleeves separately for each item. Place each item about ½″ in along either side of the main pattern piece, marked side up. Make a small red mark at the point where the sleeve will need to end in order to hold each item in place.

Mark the fold lines at the top of the checkbook and register.

2. Finish the sleeves by following Sleeves for the Inside Cover, Steps 2 through 6, on pages 15–16.

penholder

1. To make the penholder, cut a strip of fabric about 2″ wide and twice the width of the cover.

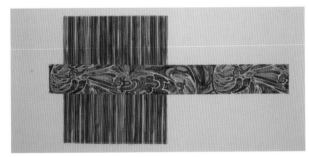

The penholder will be sewn in the center of the cover between the checkbook and register.

2. With right sides together, fold the strip in half lengthwise and stitch a narrow seam along each long side.

Make the seam as close to the edge as possible.

3. Turn this narrow pocket right side out and press. Fold the top over about 2″, press, and sew down. This is the pen pocket.

4. After the fold lines have been stitched down and the sleeves are basted in place, place the penholder along the lined center of the cover and stitch a narrow seam around the long sides and bottom. The finished pocket is flat when the cover is open, but there will be enough ease when the cover is closed to hold most pens.

Stitch penholder in place along three sides.

easy!

Use the penholder technique on your other projects. Put a penholder on the inside flap of your covered journal. For extra strength, use a small, tight zigzag stitch to reinforce the open edge of the penholder. Just make sure you allow for ease before you add your closures.

making the quilted outside

1. Place the main pattern piece on top of the batting.

2. Using your rotary cutter, cut the batting with a ½″ border around the main pattern piece.

3. Cut the center strip of fabric 2½″ by at least the open width of the cover.

4. Cut 2 highlighting strips of fabric 1″ by at least the open width of the cover.

5. Cut 2 edge strips of fabric 3½″ by at least the width of the cover.

6. Sew the fabric strips together in this order: edge, highlight, center, highlight, and edge.

Sew strips together for quilted cover.

7. Spray baste the pieced cover to the batting, trim the fabric to the edges of the batting, and quilt.

button closure

Before joining the quilted outside to the main pattern piece, mark where the button will be sewn onto the outside of the cover, with the top side up. Sew the button at this spot, using a scrap of interfacing on the backside of the quilted cover for extra stability.

Stitch button into place.

fun!

To highlight your really great button, try putting a 1″ square of one of your contrasting fabrics behind the button.

putting it all together

Follow the instructions in Putting It All Together (page 17), with one exception: after spray basting the quilted outside and lined main pattern piece, insert half of the ponytail holder between the quilted cover and the main pattern piece on the back of the cover, where the holder will stretch over the button. Edge stitching will hold the ponytail holder in place.

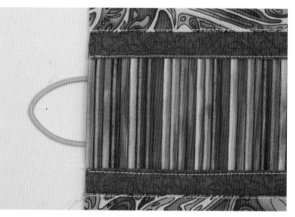

Place half of the ponytail holder at the spot where it will loop over the button.

getting it together

Follow the instructions in Rounding the Corner and Getting It Together on pages 17–18.

Variations

A. *Kaleidoscope* Swirled fabrics and a rust-colored button make this Cover Art stand out.

B. *Money Talks* What better way to decorate a checkbook cover than with money fabrics and a coin button?

C. *Love Letters* Red valentine print fabrics with a green button make this Cover Art sweet.

D. *Victorian* With majestic florals and a gold button, this Cover Art is fit for a queen!

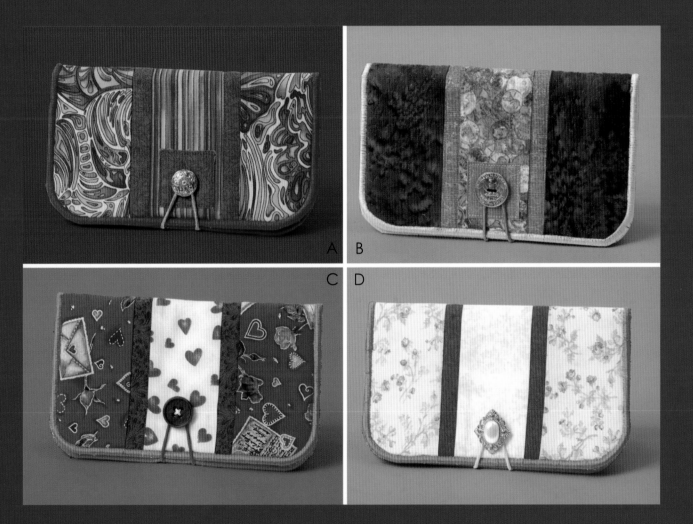

A B

C D

scrapbook cover & ribbon ties

Cover Art techniques can be used to step up the appearance of your treasured scrapbook covers, or any other book to be covered. This is where my two main hobbies—quilting and scrapbooking merge.

Paper-pieced pinecone pattern by Carol Doak

What You'll Need

- ☐ 6″ × 6″ scrapbook or larger
- ☐ 6 fat quarters (For 8½″ × 11″ or 12″ × 12″ scrapbooks, use six ½-yard cuts.)
- ☐ Invisible thread
- ☐ 1 yard of lining and sleeve fabric (For a 12″ × 12″ scrapbook, use 1½ yards.)
- ☐ ½ yard of pretty ribbon
- ☐ 1 yard regular-weight fast2fuse (This will cover even the largest scrapbooks.)
- ☐ Coordinating thread for edging
- ☐ Thread for piecing and quilting
- ☐ Basic materials (See pages 6–10.)

Girlie Girl

Thanksgiving

For the *Girlie Girl* scrapbook:

- ☐ 8½″ × 11″ post-bound scrapbook
- ☐ Metal words—Expressions from Making Memories
- ☐ Girl label—Me and My Big Ideas

For the *Thanksgiving* scrapbook:

- ☐ 6″ × 6″ post-bound scrapbook
- ☐ *Season's Change* label—Me and My Big Ideas
- ☐ 7 leaf felt stickers—Marcel Schurman Creations

How-Tos

The main technique for the embellished cover is the same as that for the basic cover. The only difference is the pieced cover and the addition of ribbon ties. Follow the instructions in Covering the Basics, until Making the Quilted Outside (pages 12–16).

easy!

As a prolific scrapbooker, I am notorious for adding pages to my albums. If you will be expanding your albums beyond their purchased size, insert the additional pages *before* measuring the outside edges and fold lines.

making the quilted outside

1. Place the main pattern piece on top of the batting.

2. Using your rotary cutter, cut the batting with roughly a ½″ border around the main pattern piece.

3. Regardless of the scrapbook size, cut a piece of fabric 7″ × 4″.

4. Stack all the fat quarters, matching 1 long edge. Trim the edge, matching to make them uniform.

5. For scrapbooks 8″ × 8″ or smaller, cut 1½″ strips from the long edge of the stack of fat quarters, ending with 24 strips about 20″ long.

> **NOTE:** For a larger album, cut 2″ strips from a stack of ½ *yards,* also ending with 24 strips, but these will be about 40″ long. This should give you enough strips to build the scrapbook cover around 2 sides of the 7″ × 4″ fabric rectangle in a chevron pattern—what I call the Lazy Girl's Logs.

6. Sew a strip of fabric to the bottom 7″ side of the fabric rectangle. Sew a matching fabric strip to the 4″ left side of the rectangle. Press and trim each strip after piecing, using the rectangle as the edge.

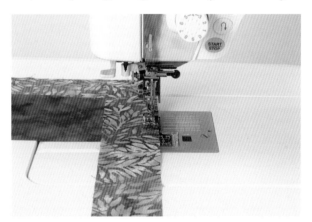

Sew matching strips to each side of the 7″ × 4″ rectangle.

easy!

Make life simple. Use a small cutting mat and ruler on your ironing board, which you have lowered and set up next to your sewing machine.

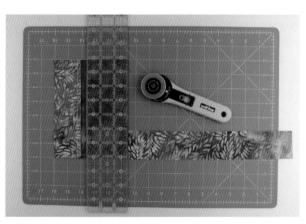

Trim strips after each piecing right on your ironing board.

7. Continue piecing the strips, changing colors with each row, until the pieced fabric covers the bottom edge of your batting. When you reach the bottom, you will still have space on what will be the back of the cover that needs to be filled. Continue piecing vertical strips across the back until the batting is covered.

Work from the upper right of the cover to the bottom edge.

8. Spray baste the pieced cover to the batting, and quilt as desired.

adding embellishments, beads & doodads

I prefer embellishments that can be sewn onto the quilted outside. Sometimes these embellishments are made from fabric, like the label on the *Thanksgiving* cover. Some metal embellishments have holes that allow you to sew them onto the quilted cover. Other embellishments, such as the metal words I used in the *Girlie Girl* scrapbook cover, also lend themselves to being sewn into place. If the embellishment is heavy, use a scrap of interfacing behind the cover to add stability to the sewing. Regardless of what is added onto the cover, all sewn embellishments need to be attached to the quilted outside before it is joined to the rest of the cover pieces.

> **NOTE:** I define *heavy* as a weight greater than that of two quarters.

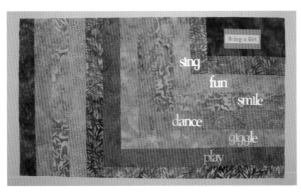

Embellishments on the *Girlie Girl* cover were simple to sew down using invisible thread.

The exception to embellishing before joining the pieces is in the case of embellishments that need to be glued down. This is done after everything else is completed on the album. Be careful not to let strings of glue mar your finished cover and try not to glue down any heavy embellishment that might eventually pull and tear the cover.

Most ribbons will fray at the ends. Use a tiny bit of FrayBlock or a similar product to prevent this. (See Sources, page 48.)

making ribbon ties

Before joining the quilted outside to the main pattern piece, place half the ribbon between the outside and the main pattern piece on either side of the cover's edges. The spray baste will temporarily hold the ribbons in place, but be careful not to move them too soon.

Place ribbons between cover and main pattern piece before joining.

Gently pull the ribbons taut while the machine stitches over them. When you're not stitching near the ribbons, keep them out of the way.

putting it all together

Follow the instructions for Putting It All Together, Rounding the Corner, and Getting It Together (pages 17–18).

Variations

A. ***Africa*** Kerin Martin takes you to the savanna with her photo album Cover Art.

B. ***China Reflections*** Phyllis Jones covered a small scrapbook/photo album with a blue Chinese-style print.

C. ***O Tannenbaum*** This Christmas tree uses winter brights to convey the feeling of the season.

D. ***Holiday in Paris*** Sam Hunter used photos she took on vacation to decorate her Cover Art.

E. ***Baby Photo Album*** for Lauren Lynn Shortt used a Log Cabin heart to show the love that went into this.

F. ***Loose Disc*** Annie Toth keeps her CDs handy in this CD case.

flapped journal

There are few things in life more personal than a journal. Covering and decorating your journal (or anyone else's) in a way that sings to your soul is as simple as Cover Art.

What You'll Need

- Journal (My journal is 8¾″ × 5⅝″ and was $4 on the bookstore discount table.)

- 10 strips of fabric, 2″ x 21″—of similar aqua shades (for Under the Sea journal) or black and white fabrics (Brighten My Day locked journal)—cut into 2″ squares. Yields at least 90 squares. (In the end I used 88 squares.)

- 1 yard of coordinating fabric for lining and sleeves

- 2″ strip of ¾″-wide hook-and-loop tape

- ½ yard of ½″-wide satin ribbon

- Desired embellishments

- ½ yard regular-weight fast2fuse

- Coordinating thread for edging

- Thread for piecing and quilting

- Basic materials (See pages 6–10.)

How-Tos

main pattern piece

1. Follow the instructions for making the main pattern piece (pages 12–13) through Step 3.

2. To make the side edges, carefully overlap the right side onto the front of the journal to make what will be the flap, keeping it almost tight to the book. With a black pen, mark the left edge on the main pattern piece and the right edge where you want the flap to end. This mark should be at least 2″ from the right edge of the journal.

> **NOTE:** The basic design includes a flapped cover. Two variations are shown, one with a hook-and-loop-tape closure and one with a mini-lock closure—which is more for decoration than privacy.

3. With a ruler, draw black edge lines where each small mark is, using the top and bottom edges to square off each side of the main pattern piece. Repeat for the opposite side. Use your rotary cutter to cut ½″ away from the edge line on each side.

Wrap the main pattern piece around the journal, overlapping the right side onto the front.

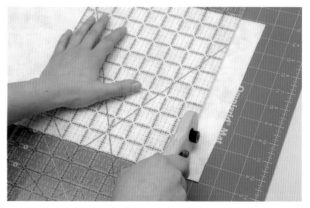

Mark and trim ½″ away from the edge line, including at the edge of the flap.

Under the Sea

fold lines & cover lining

1. Follow the instructions on pages 14–15 for marking and making the fold lines, through Step 8.

2. Fold lines also need to be made for the flap. Stretch the flap onto the front of the cover and mark fold lines where the cover will stretch over the side of the book, as was done for the other fold lines.

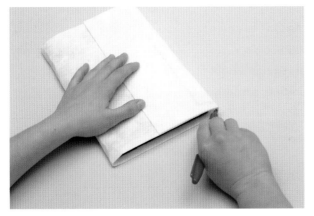

Stretch the flap over the side of the book and mark where the fold lines should be stitched.

3. Place the ironed lining fabric wrong side up on the table. Place the main pattern piece, marked side up, on the fabric, along the selvage width.

4. Cut the lining fabric around the main pattern piece, leaving about a 1″ border. (See photos on pages 12–13 as a guide.)

5. Bring both pieces together to the ironing board and fuse the lining fabric to the main pattern piece.

6. Trim the fabric to the edge of the main pattern piece. Stitch along each marked fold line.

sleeves

1. The flap prevents the inside right sleeve from being stitched down along the outside edge. Make the left sleeve according to Sleeves for the Inside Cover, Steps 1 through 4, on page 15.

2. For the right sleeve, measure the inside cover area where the right side cover of the journal will sit.

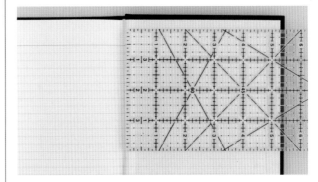

Measure from edge to edge of the inside cover area.

3. Cut a piece of sleeve fabric twice as wide and 2″ longer than the inside cover area.

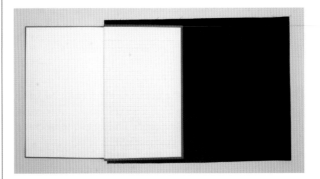

4. With right sides together, stitch a seam along the length of the right sleeve, ½″ in from the edge. Turn the tube right side out and press with the seam in the middle of the tube.

The seam is pressed along the middle of the sleeve.

5. Pin this sleeve into place inside the right cover, making sure that the sleeve is not covering the journal's fold, with the edges hanging over the top and bottom of the main pattern piece.

Don't place the right sleeve where it will get in the way of the journal's binding or the flap on the main pattern piece.

6. With the marked side facing up, carefully baste stitch the sleeves to the main pattern piece, about ⅛″ from the edge, making sure the sleeves do not shift. Trim the sleeves to the edge of the main pattern piece.

making the quilted outside

1. Place the main pattern piece on top of the batting.

2. Using your rotary ruler, cut the batting with a ½″ border around the main pattern piece.

3. Arrange the 2″ squares over the cut batting and sew them together row by row, until the finished piece is large enough to cover the batting.

4. Spray baste the pieced outside to the batting, and quilt. Trim, embellish, and join to the main pattern piece and sleeves.

hook-and-loop-tape closure

1. To make the hook-and-loop-tape closure on the flap, cut a piece of self-stick hook-and-loop tape about 2″ shorter than the length of the book.

2. Fold the cover around the journal to get the placement as accurate as possible. Stick the hook-and-loop tape into place with one piece along the inside flap and the other piece on the edge of the quilted outside, allowing for a little ease once the journal is inside. Add the hook-and-loop tape **before** the quilted outside is joined to the main pattern piece.

3. Once the hook-and-loop tape is in place, separate the pieces and stitch the edges of the tape down.

locked closure

☐ Extra-small D-ring (from the sewing notions aisle of your fabric store)

☐ Small luggage lock and key

1. On the quilted outside cover, sew a small D-ring to the area that will rest under the flap. With a piece of regular-weight fast2fuse on the underside of the batting, securely sew the D-ring in place.

Sew D-ring into place.

2. After the cover is completely sewn together, mark where the D-ring will need to come through the flap. Sew a buttonhole at this spot on the flap, cut it open, and slide the D-ring through the hole. Now you can use your small luggage lock on the D-ring closure.

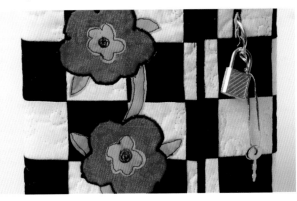

ribbon bookmark

1. Cut the ribbon length in half to make 2 pieces, ¼ yard × ½″. Press if wrinkled.

2. Place the ribbon between the quilted outside and the main pattern piece at the top of the cover where the journal's binding will sit.

3. Thread beads onto the ends of the ribbon to decorate and add weight. Tie a simple square knot below the beads to hold them in place.

putting it all together

Follow the instructions in Putting It All Together on page 17.

rounding the corner & getting it together

Follow the instructions in Rounding the Corner and Getting It Together on pages 17–18.

Variations

A. ***Fields of Pansies*** I used a ribbon flap to keep this cover closed. The ribbon is threaded through two buttonholes made to the ribbon's width.

B. ***You Are My Sunshine*** On this one, I chose a hook-and-loop-tape closure.

A

B

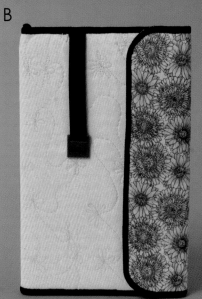

sketchbook with
pencil holder

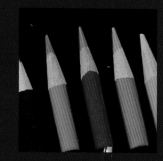

Start your creative expressions with Cover Art devoted to creativity. A sketchbook cover with a handy panel designed to hold those wonderful colored pencils or art markers will bring a smile to the face of any artist tired of looking for drawing tools.

What You'll Need

- ☐ 6″ × 9″ spiral-bound sketchbook
- ☐ A pack of 12 or more art pencils
- ☐ ½ yard of cover material
- ☐ 1 yard of lining and sleeve fabric
- ☐ 5 coordinating fabric scraps, each about 5″ square
- ☐ ½ yard lightweight fusible interfacing
- ☐ ½ yard regular-weight fast2fuse (This will cover even the largest sketchbooks.)
- ☐ Coordinating thread for edging
- ☐ Thread for piecing and quilting
- ☐ Scrapbook embellishments (I used Emotions Washer Words by Making Memories.)
- ☐ 1 yard of ribbon
- ☐ Stiletto, bamboo skewer, or other long, thin tool
- ☐ Basic materials (See pages 6–10.)

> **NOTE: You will need a zipper foot for your sewing machine to make the art pencil sleeves in this cover.**

fun!

Many sketchbooks open from the bottom instead of the side. To adapt the cover for this design, simply turn the pad, and your imagination, on its side. Your pencil panel will flip over and cover the front of the sketchbook when closed.

How-Tos

main pattern piece

Follow the instructions for the main pattern piece through Step 6 (on pages 12–13), with one exception: in Step 6, after you've marked the edges with the red pen and you're preparing to cut, add a ½″ allowance to one side and 1½″ to the other side. This will give you enough ease for the art pencil sleeves.

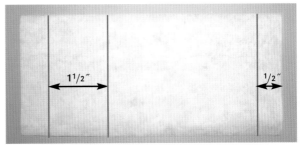

Mark 1½″ extra along one side to accommodate the art pencils.

fold lines & cover lining

1. Because you have allowed an extra 1″ in the center of the cover for the space needed to hold the art pencils, fold your main pattern piece in half where the cover will fold when finished and mark the exact center.

2. Open and draw the centerline using your rotary ruler. Then draw lines on both sides of the centerline, spaced about a ¼″ apart, for about 1″ on each side.

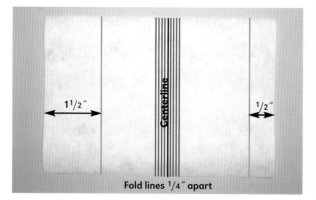

Sewing 2″ of fold lines will give your cover plenty of bending space.

3. Continue following Fold Lines & Cover Lining, Steps 4 through 8, on pages 14–15.

sketchbook sleeve for the inside cover

The sketchbook cover will have only 1 sleeve, on the inner right side of the cover. The inner left side will be used for the art pencil sleeves.

1. Place the sketchbook on the right lined side of the open main pattern piece, leaving a ½″ border around the top, bottom, and right edges of the sketchbook. Make a small mark at the edge where the sleeve will need to end in order to hold the sketchbook in place.

2. Finish the sleeve by following Sleeves for the Inside Cover, Steps 2 through 6, on pages 15–16.

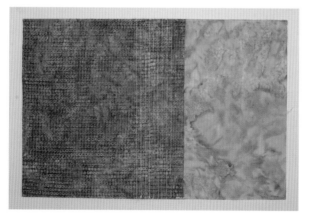

Make only one sleeve for the sketchbook cover.

art pencil sleeves

These instructions can be tricky, so take them slowly.

1. Measure the length of 1 of the pencils that will be held in the sleeve.

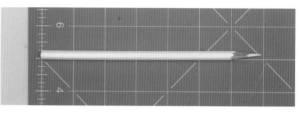

Pencil length will determine sleeve length.

2. Measure the width of the left inside main pattern piece, up to where the cover will bend at the fold lines.

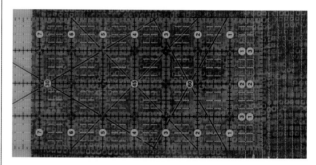

Measure to the cover's bend.

3. Measure and cut a piece of sleeve fabric **double the length** of the pencil and **double the width** of the inner left side of the main pattern piece.

Doubling the width gives enough ease for the pencils.

4. Using the cut sleeve as a pattern, cut a piece the same size from the lightweight fusible interfacing.

The interfacing adds structure to the pencil sleeves and makes a great-looking finished cover.

5. Fuse the interfacing to the wrong side of the sleeve, following the manufacturer's instructions.

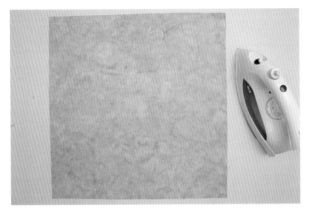

Some interfacings require steam or a pressing cloth. Read the manufacturer's instructions.

6. Fold the pencil sleeve in half widthwise, trim 1˝ from the open edge, and press firmly.

7. Stay stitch about ½˝ in from the folded edge of the sleeve.

fun!

This is a perfect place to use your machine's decorative stitches!

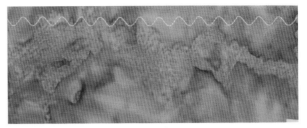

Have fun with your machine's settings!

8. At what will be the sleeve's right side, fold the doubled fabric under ½˝, press, and sew.

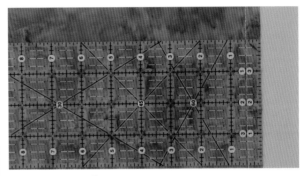

Turn under ½˝ and sew to help make a clean fold.

9. Square the pencil sleeve fabric to the main pattern piece by making sure the folded edge is parallel to the top edge of the main pattern piece and the bottom edge of the sleeve fabric drops about 1˝ below the bottom edge of the main pattern piece.

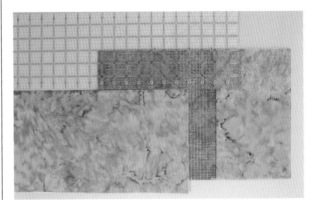

Your rotary ruler will come in handy again for ensuring straight lines.

10. Sew the pencil sleeves' right side edge onto the inside main pattern piece just to the outside of the left side's bend. Trim the excess fabric from the inside carefully.

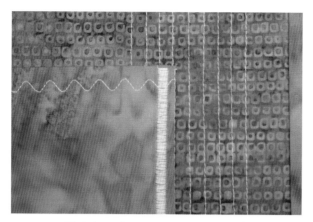

Tack down the top using a zigzag stitch.

11. Take 1 of your art pencils and tuck it between the main pattern piece and the art pencil sleeve fabric.

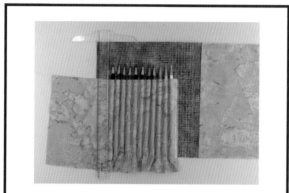

NOTE: T-square rulers are very helpful for lining up pieces. After you place each pencil under the sleeve, use the T-square ruler to measure the distance from the top edge of the main pattern piece to the folded edge of the pencil sleeve. Keep the measurement the same with each new pencil sleeve.

12. With the zipper foot on your machine, sew a line from the top of the sleeve to the bottom, as close to the edge of the pencil as possible, while holding the pencil in place. In other words, you are sewing the pencil *into* the sleeve, with a seam on the side.

fast!

Backstitch at least ½″ from the folded edge to secure your sleeves' stitching.

13. Repeat this step for the rest of the pencils, or until you reach within 1″ of the left edge of the main pattern piece.

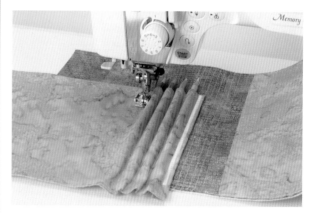

Stitch slowly and carefully along each pencil sleeve to avoid creating uneven sleeves.

14. Stitch baste the far left side of the pencil sleeve to the main pattern piece. Trim the left side of the pencil sleeve to the edge of the main pattern piece.

Basting along the open edge will keep the sleeve in place when you sew everything together.

15. Remove the pencils and carefully press the bottom edge of the art pencil sleeves 1 sleeve at a time. Don't press the sleeves in a direction. Try to press them flat down. If you have trouble getting them flat, use something long and thin to make them obey, like a bamboo skewer, stiletto, or tube turner.

Do this carefully for a much nicer-looking finish.

16. Baste the art pencil sleeves ⅛″ from the bottom edge. Trim the fabric to the edges of the cover.

Baste ⅛″ from the bottom edge to secure your sleeves.

fun!

The number of pencils your cover can hold is dependent upon your sketchbook. The 6″ × 9″ sketchbook I used held a dozen pencils easily.

making the quilted outside

1. Place the main pattern piece on top of the batting.

2. With your rotary ruler, cut the batting with about a ½″ border around the main pattern piece.

3. Cut 5 rectangles, 1½″ × 4½″, from the coordinating scraps. Sew them together along the long edges in a row.

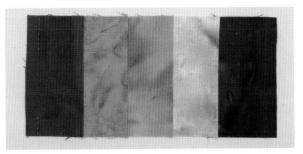

Sew the scrap rectangles together in a row.

4. Using the batting as a guide, cut a wide strip of fabric from the cover material, 5½″ wide by the length of the batting.

5. Cut 3″ from the top of the strip, leaving a rectangle 5½″ × 3″.

> NOTE: Because your sketchbook may have different dimensions, I can only give you a guide for the cuts. Adjust accordingly.

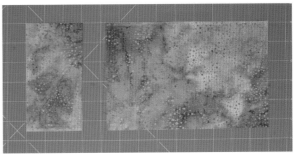

Cut 3″ from the top of the strip.

6. Cut 3 pieces of ribbon about 5″ long. Take 3 washer embellishments, string a piece of ribbon through each one, and position them so each washer drops down onto a section of the pieced row. Pin in place.

Carefully position and pin your embellishments in place.

7. Carefully sew the pieced row to the 3″ × 5½″ rectangle along the 5½″ side, making sure the stitches secure the edges of the ribbons. Press the seam toward the rectangle.

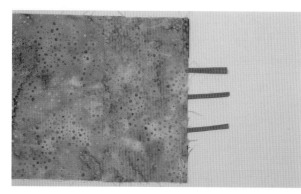

Make sure your stitching secures the ribbon.

8. Sew the leftover rectangle of fabric to the bottom of the pieced row.

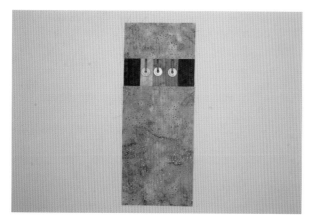

Strip is now finished.

9. Using the cut batting as a guide, measure how far in from the front right edge of the cover you want the just-pieced strip to rest. Cut a strip of cover material to that size and sew it to the right side of the strip.

10. Repeat for the left side, measuring across the back of the cover to the left edge.

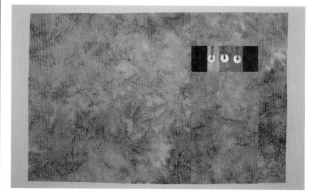

Material will now cover the entire piece of batting.

11. Spray baste the pieced cover to the batting, and quilt as desired.

putting it all together & rounding the corner

Follow the instructions in Putting It All Together and Rounding the Corner, on page 17.

getting it together

Follow the instructions for Getting It Together, on page 18, with one exception: leave the inside cover up for both passes of your zigzag edge stitching. The pencil sleeves make it difficult to sew from the front side.

Variations

A. *Imagine, Create, Inspire* has twelve pencil pockets.

B. *Spirit* has just nine pencil pockets.

C. & D. *Imagine, Create, Delight* took 2nd place in the 2006 Hoffman Challenge!

Photos by Kelly Gallagher-Abbott of the Hoffman Challenge

about the author

Jake Finch started sewing in 1987 when she gave up her credit cards—but not her love of new clothes. In 2000, while pregnant with her daughter and craving participation in the sacred sisterhood of the fiber addicted, Jake joined her first guild and mini-group. Along the way she discovered scrapbooks. Bringing together her love of paper, words, and pictures and presenting them in an attractive manner made her journalist's heart sing—and her husband sigh at his wife's new addiction.

Married to Stephen for 20 years, Jake lives in Simi Valley, California, with their daughter, Samantha, and two cats. She loves to hear from others who share her obsessions; she can be reached at www.jakefinchdesigns.com.

sources

The materials used in this book were all easily located at quilt, scrapbook, and craft stores, including online sources. Companies can also be contacted directly for orders or retail referrals.

505 Spray and Fix
Temporary, repositionable spray adhesive
J.T. Trading Corp.
860-350-5565
www.sprayandfix.com

Bubble Jet Set 2000
Allows you to print directly on fabric with an ink- or a bubble-jet printer
C. Jenkins Company
314-521-7544
www.cjenkinscompany.com

fast2fuse Double-Sided Fusible Interfacing
Helps make Cover Art fast, fun & easy!
C&T Publishing
800-284-1114
www.fast2fuse.com

FranklinCovey
It was one of this company's binder products that set me on the path to covering the world.
800-819-1812
www.franklincovey.com

FrayBlock
Prevents fabric and ribbon from fraying.
June Tailor
800-844-5400
www.junetailor.com

Fray Check
Liquid seam sealant
Prym Consumer USA
www.dritz.com

Levenger
A wonderful source for top-quality journals, notebooks, index cards, and other writing papers.
800-544-0880
www.levenger.com

Making Memories
Great scrapbook supplies for that can easily be used for Cover Art projects (available at most large craft retailers and scrapbook stores)
800-286-5263
www.makingmemories.com

Marcel Schurman
Makers of an expansive line of unique and diverse paper products
www.papyrusonline.com

Me & My Big Ideas
More great scrapbook supplies that can be used for Cover Art projects (available at most large craft retailers and scrapbook stores)
www.meandmybigideas.com

Printed Treasures
A soft fabric that gives you sharp, lasting images from any ink-jet printer
Milliken & Company
866-787-8458
www.printedtreasures.com

Robison-Anton Textile Company
Thread for machine embroidery and quilting
201-941-0500
www.robison-anton.com

Schmetz
This website helps you determine what type of needles work best with what types of threads and fabrics.
www.schmetz.com

Stitch Witchery
Fusible bonding web
Prym Consumer USA
www.dritz.com

Superior Threads
Thread for machine embellishing and quilting
800-499-1777
www.superiorthreads.com

The Warm Company
Makers of Steam-a-Seam 2, and Warm & Natural and Warm & White batting
800-234-WARM
www.warmcompany.com

YLI
Threads for machine embellishing and quilting
803-985-3100
www.ylicorp.com